Relax Range Book 1
Dojo of Peace

Recharge Publishing

ISBN: **1537632477**
ISBN-13: **978-1537632476**

DEDICATION

Firstly to my two besties, who I love so much and then to you for taking charge and giving yourself 5 minutes peace!
Enjoy!.

CONTENTS

MESSAGE FOR YOU

Life can be crazy sometimes and we often don't think about ourselves as much as we should each day. Whether it's a job, family, illness or something else, all things that take up your time and energy each day. To be the best in any situation you need to be focused and it's to easy to just go through the motions of the day each day. Take 5 minutes just for yourself! Recharge and go for it again. Your loved ones and your sole will thank you for it..

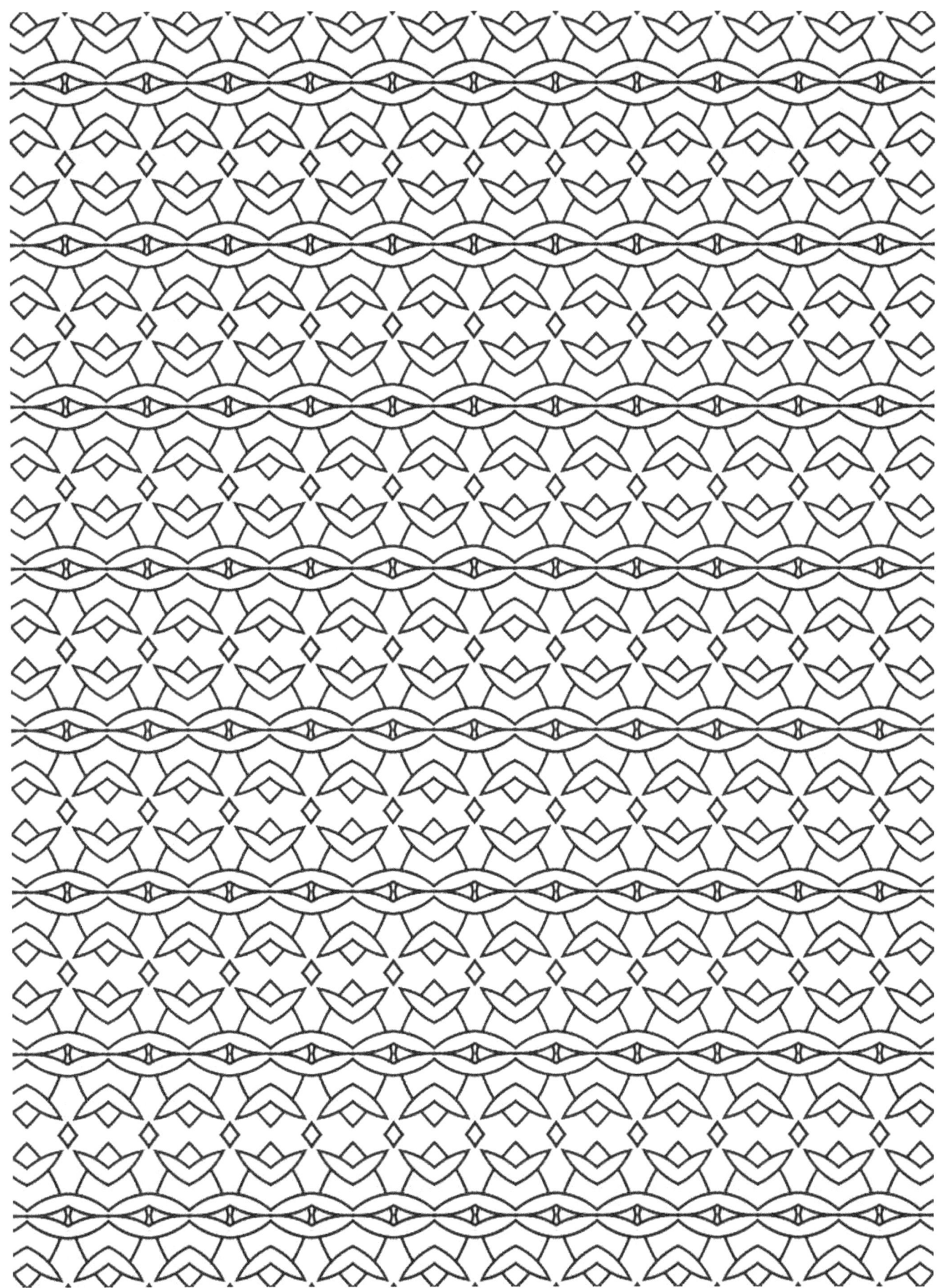

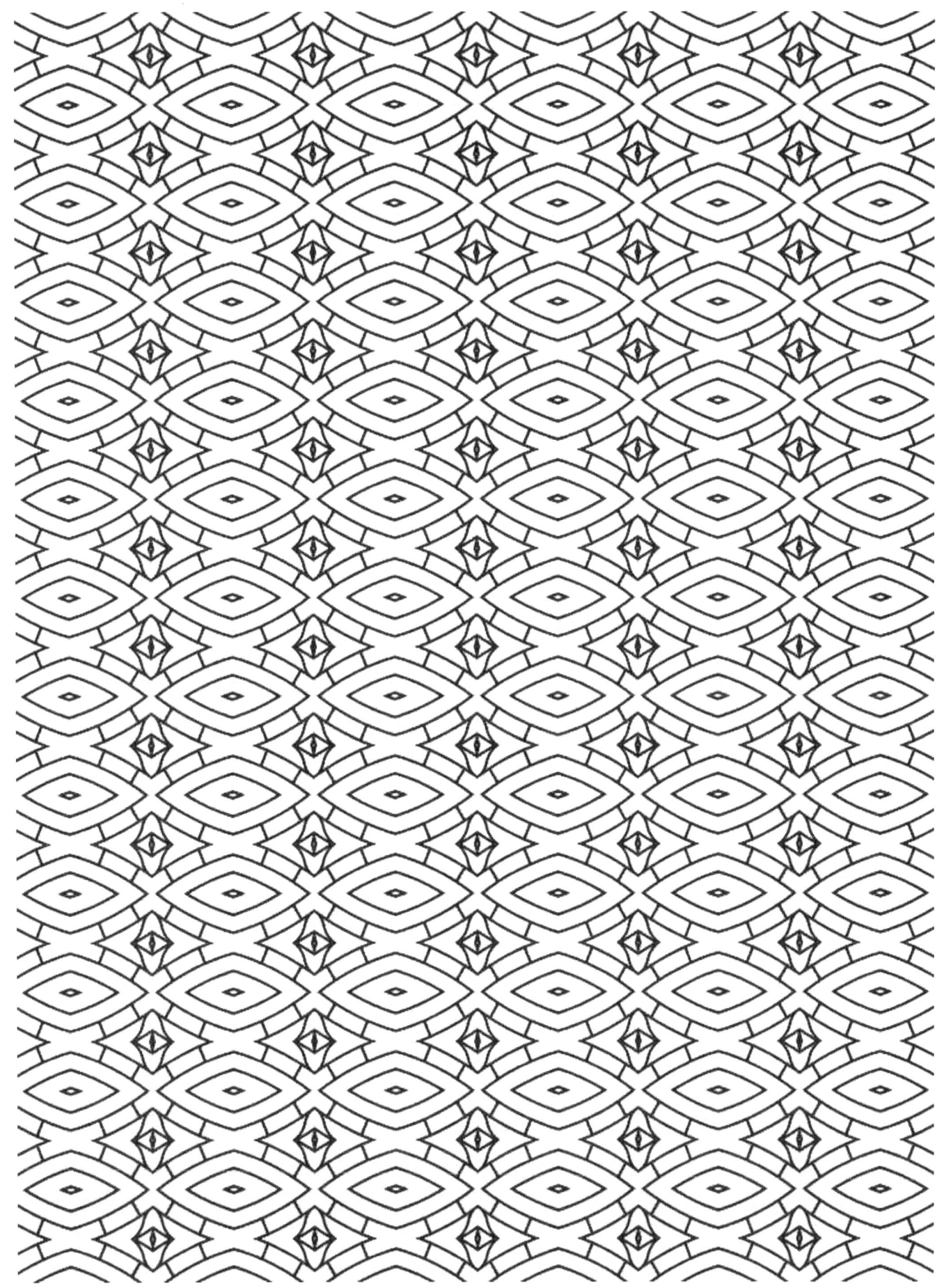

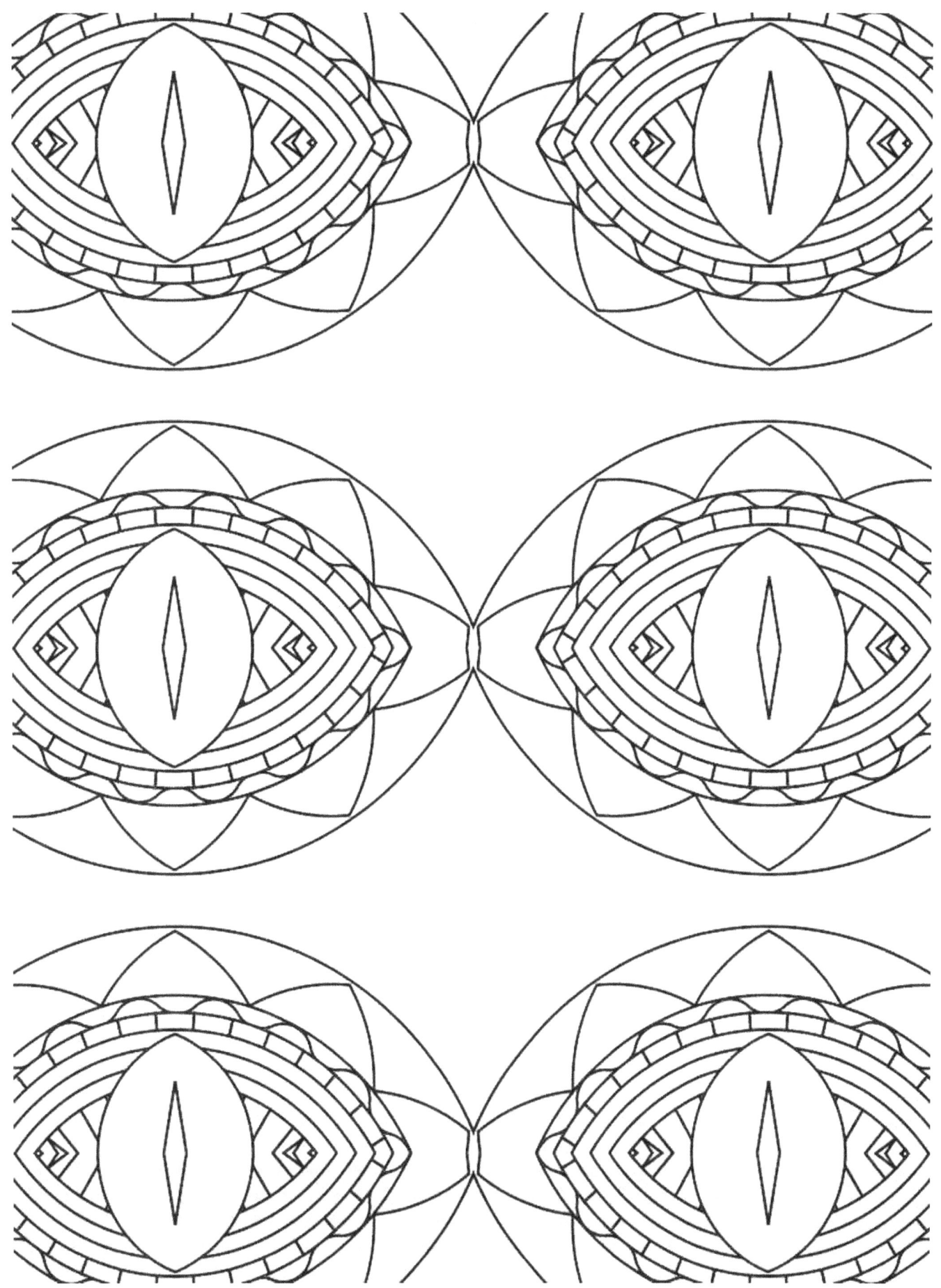

THANKS

I hope you have enjoyed this book and it has brought you some peace through out your day.
I understand how crazy life can be sometimes so it's important to take 5 minutes everyday just for yourself, I hope
this book has given you some comfort and a renewed sense of focus.

If you would like to receive a free download printable coloring book please use this link, just enter your name and
an email address I can send your for book to. Thanks again.

http://bit.ly/2cTSkyk